ANCIENT EGYPT

Amanda Martin

Hello, I'm Hunefer

My name
is Esmut

Come and explore
MY WORLD and
find out what it's like
to live in ancient Egypt.

I'm called Tamyt

World Book

First published in the United States and Canada by
World Book Inc.
525 W. Monroe
Chicago, IL 60661
in association with Two-Can Publishing Ltd.

© Two-Can Publishing Ltd., 1997

**For information on other World Book products, call 1-800-255-1750, x 2238,
or visit us at our Web site at http://www.worldbook.com**

Editor: Clare Oliver
Art direction and design: Helen McDonagh
Text: Amanda Martin
Consultant: Delia Pemberton
Cover design: Helen Holmes
Senior Commissioning Editor: Jacqueline McCann
Managing Editor: Christine Morley
Managing Art Director: Carole Orbell
Model maker: Melanie Williams
Illustrator: David Hitch
Photography: John Englefield
Special thanks to: Melissa Tucker, World Book Publishing

Library of Congress Cataloging-in-Publication Data
Martin, Amanda.
    Ancient Egypt / Amanda Martin.
       p.   cm. — (My world)
    Includes index.
    Summary: While telling about her life in ancient Egypt, nine-year
 -old Hunefer includes information about families, homes, food,
clothing, fun and games, travel, beliefs, and burial practices.
   ISBN 0-7166-9414-X. — ISBN 0-7166-9415-8 (pbk.)
   1. Egypt—Civilization—To 332 B.C.—Juvenile literature.
 [1. Egypt—Civilization—To 322 B.C.]   I. Title. II. Series: My world (Chicago, III.)
 DT61.M346 1997
 932—dc21   97-3532

Printed in Hong Kong

3 4 5 6 7 8 9 10 01 00 99

CONTENTS

My people

My name is Hunefer and I'm nine years old. I live in Thebes, which is a city next to the river Nile in Egypt. If you look at the map, you can see Thebes just by the bend in the river.

About my country

Egypt is a hot, dry country, so all the villages and towns are close to the river. The capital of Egypt is Thebes. It is famous for its great temples and tombs. Tombs are where important people are buried. The most important person in all Egypt is the king. We call him the pharaoh, and believe he is a living god.

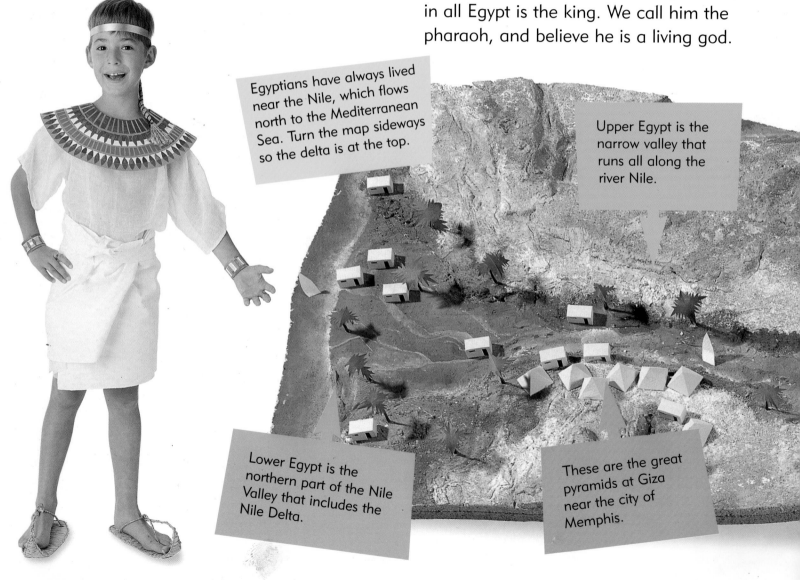

Egyptians have always lived near the Nile, which flows north to the Mediterranean Sea. Turn the map sideways so the delta is at the top.

Upper Egypt is the narrow valley that runs all along the river Nile.

Lower Egypt is the northern part of the Nile Valley that includes the Nile Delta.

These are the great pyramids at Giza near the city of Memphis.

Along the river Nile

My father says that without the Nile, no one could live in Egypt. Every summer, the Nile floods and waters the soil. It also spreads a rich black mud over the land where we plant our crops. We call this fertile area Kemet, which means "the black land."

Symbols used on the map

Kemet, or the black land

villages, towns, and cities

pyramids and tombs

I live here in Thebes. The pharaoh lives in Thebes, too.

In your time...
Over 3,000 years ago, in Hunefer's time, Thebes was the capital of Egypt. Cairo, which is next to the ancient town of Memphis, is the capital today.

Deshret is a dry area of land where only a few plants can grow.

The red land

The farther you go from the Nile, the drier the land becomes, until it's just desert. We call it Deshret, which means "the red land." Not many people live there, but lots of useful things are found there. Many years ago, stone from Deshret was used to build the pyramids.

My family

I live at home with my parents and my sister Tamyt. We have lots of servants living in our house, including Esmut. She's seven – the same age as Tamyt. Not everyone in Egypt has servants. We do because my father is a nobleman and works for the pharaoh.

At school, I practice writing on these scrolls. They're made from a type of paper called papyrus.

My father's work

My father is an important man. He's the pharaoh's chief writer, or scribe. One of his jobs is to watch over the other scribes, and sometimes he has to go to the temple to work as a priest. When I grow up, I'll work at the royal court like my father. That's why I go to school, so I can learn to become a scribe.

Let's make an ostrich-feather fan

Find thick cardboard, scissors, pencil, ruler, tape, broom handle, paints, paintbrush, white paper, pink tissue paper, glue, fluffy trim.

1 Cut some cardboard into a semicircle with a straight edge 5 in. (12 cm) long. Tape the cardboard to one end of the broom handle. Paint the handle and the cardboard.

2 Cut 4 sheets of tissue paper, 12 in. x 4 in. (30 cm x 10 cm). Glue them together and sandwich between 2 sheets of white paper. Only glue down the middle of each piece of paper. Make 6 bundles.

3 Draw a feather shape on each of the 6 bundles of paper. Cut out the shapes and cut around the edges. Fluff out the edges and paint as shown.

4 Glue the feathers to the back of the cardboard on the handle. Decorate the fan with fluffy trim.

My mother's work

My mother looks after our house and tells all the servants what to do. When she's not at home, my mother works at the royal court. She's in charge of looking after the queen's clothes, and making sure the "Great Royal Wife" always looks her best.

My sister

Girls in Egypt don't go to school, so my sister Tamyt stays at home, and my mother teaches her how to run a household. Even after her chores, Tamyt still has plenty of free time to play with Esmut or with her toys.

Our friend Esmut

Esmut is our youngest servant, and she's also our friend. Most of the time, Esmut works in the kitchen, running errands for the cook and helping to wash the dishes. When she's finished, Esmut keeps Tamyt company. They play games together, and when it's really hot, Esmut fans Tamyt to keep her cool.

Esmut uses an ostrich-feather fan to keep Tamyt cool.

Tamyt still plays with toys. Her favorite is this cat with a snapping mouth.

7

Our house

Our house is one of the biggest in Thebes. Tamyt and I even have our own bedrooms, but Esmut has to share with the other servants. Most homes in Egypt are built of mud. The mud is shaped into bricks, which are left to dry in the sun. Mud-brick houses don't last forever, but it doesn't matter. When the bricks start to crumble, we knock down the house and build a new one.

I go to sleep with my head on a headrest. It keeps my neck cool while I'm sleeping.

In your time...
Headrests are still used in many African countries. They are mostly made of wood, as they were in ancient Egypt.

Let's make a headrest

Find 3 cardboard tubes 2 in. (5 cm) in diameter, scissors, tape, stiff cardboard, newspaper, flour, water, a tablespoon of salt, paint, paintbrush.

1 Cut a tube 4½ in. (11 cm) long, and the others 5½ in. (14 cm) long. Cut a piece of cardboard 4 in. x 12 in. (10 cm x 30 cm). Tape tubes to it.

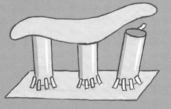

2 Cut a piece of cardboard 4 in. x 14 in. (10 cm x 35 cm). Round off the corners. Bend it and tape it to the top of the tubes.

3 Mix flour, salt, and water into a thin paste. Tear the newspaper into pieces and dip them in the paste. Cover the headrest with about 4 layers.

4 Let the headrest dry. Paint it white. Let it dry, then paint it gold.

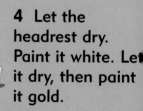

8

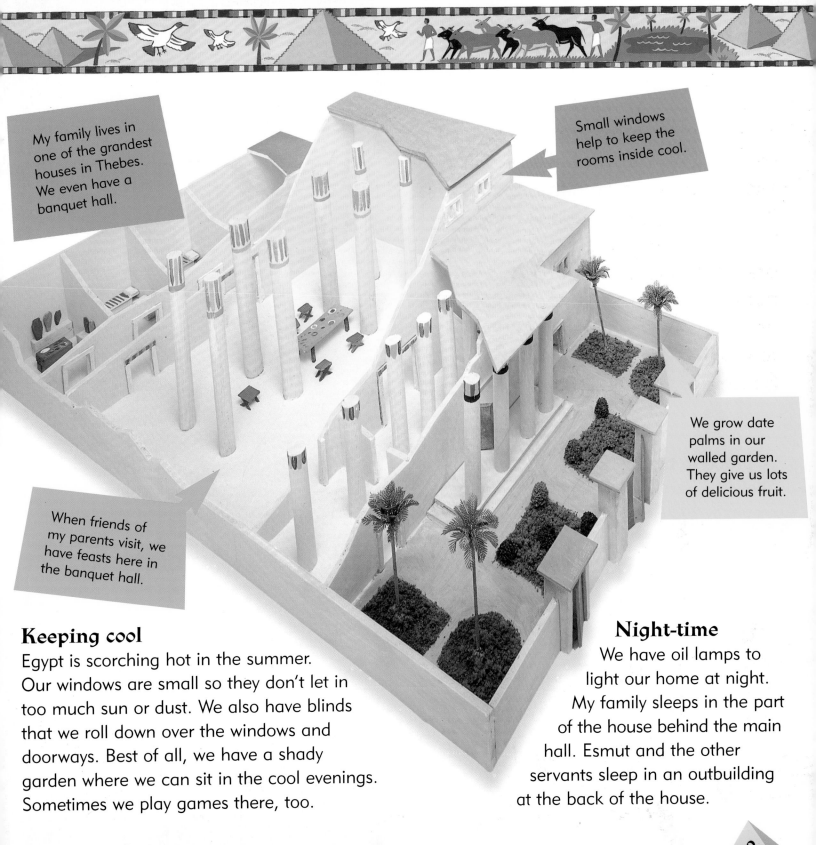

My family lives in one of the grandest houses in Thebes. We even have a banquet hall.

Small windows help to keep the rooms inside cool.

When friends of my parents visit, we have feasts here in the banquet hall.

We grow date palms in our walled garden. They give us lots of delicious fruit.

Keeping cool

Egypt is scorching hot in the summer. Our windows are small so they don't let in too much sun or dust. We also have blinds that we roll down over the windows and doorways. Best of all, we have a shady garden where we can sit in the cool evenings. Sometimes we play games there, too.

Night-time

We have oil lamps to light our home at night. My family sleeps in the part of the house behind the main hall. Esmut and the other servants sleep in an outbuilding at the back of the house.

Life in Thebes

My city, Thebes, is the most important place in Egypt because our ruler, the pharaoh, lives here. All the buildings in the city are built on high land. This is so they don't get washed away every year when the river Nile bursts its banks.

Each morning, our cook sends Esmut to the market for fresh food.

A place to trade

Thebes is a busy place, and its streets are always crowded. Boats dock here all the time, bringing people from other towns along the Nile with goods to trade at the market.

At the market, we trade grain for the things we need.

Going shopping

Everyone in Thebes meets to trade in the market place. You can swap, or barter, all kinds of things, maybe a fish for a headrest, or a goose for some wine. We send Esmut to do the shopping early in the morning. She sets off shortly after sunrise, when it's still quite cool.

The streets of Thebes

My grandparents and most of my aunts and uncles live in houses very close to ours. Tamyt and I often play with our cousins. To visit them, we walk down narrow, crooked streets, through crowds of people and animals.

The houses have flat roofs. People sleep up here when it's hot.

The buildings in Thebes are painted white to reflect the heat of the sun.

People store their food and wine in shady cellars to keep them cool.

The food we eat

Esmut usually brings back all sorts of fresh fruit from the market. The ones I like best are pomegranates and grapes. Tamyt and I are lucky that we have lots of delicious things to eat, including fish from the Nile and fresh meat. Most Egyptians cannot afford to buy meat to eat.

Esmut is wearing a perfume cone on her head. It drips scented oil on to her wig and leaves a lovely smell.

Food for a feast

We have lots of feasts at my house. Esmut brings food to the table on gold and silver dishes. We eat meat such as roast sheep and geese, and drink sweet wine. For dessert there's fruit and sticky fig treats made with honey.

At a feast, Tamyt and I eat at low tables. We use our fingers to pick up the food.

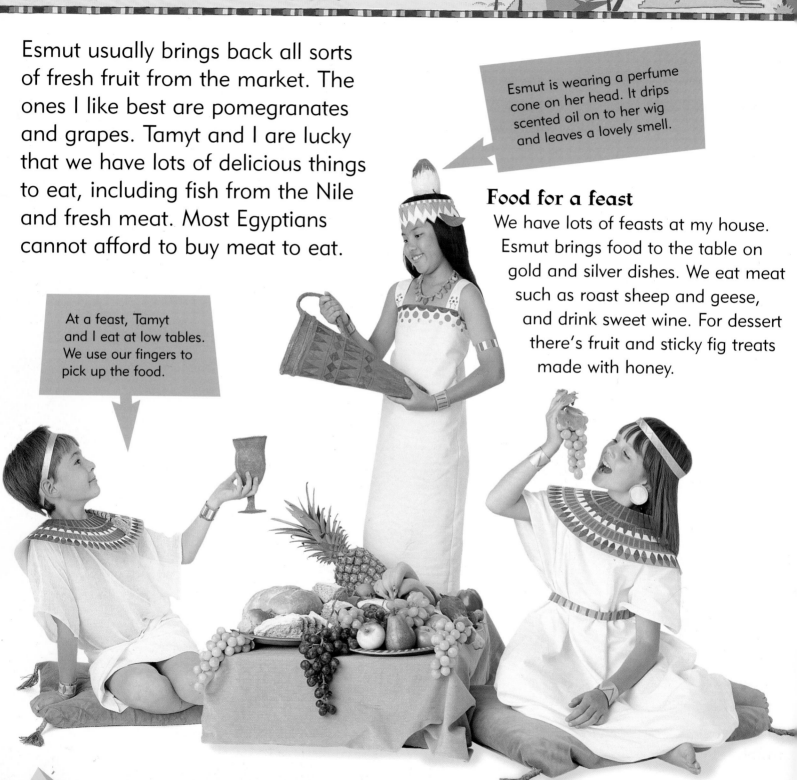

Bread for us all

Everyone in Egypt, rich or poor, eats bread. Sometimes it's flavored with herbs, honey, or dates. A lot of grit is added by accident, too. It gets into the grain while it's being ground into flour. My grandmother's teeth have been almost worn away from eating gritty bread!

Oxen trample the wheat to separate the grain from the outer husk, or chaff.

Cooking outside

We have a kitchen in our house, but most people cook outside or on the rooftops. It's far too hot to cook indoors, and there's also the danger that the rest of the house might catch fire.

Let's make sticky fig treats

Adult help needed

Find 1¾ oz. (50 g) almonds, 1¾ oz. (50 g) walnuts, 4 fresh figs, 1 tsp ground cardamom, water, honey, blender, knife, 2 plates, spoon.

1 Ask an adult to grind the almonds into tiny pieces, in the blender. Do the same with the walnuts. Keep the two types of nut separate.

2 Wash the figs and slice off the ends. Coarsely chop the fruit.

3 Put the figs, walnuts, and cardamom in the blender with a little water. Blend together, adding more water if the mixture is too sticky.

4 Spoon the mixture onto a clean work surface. Shape it into little balls.

5 Roll the balls first in honey and then in the chopped almonds. Now enjoy!

The clothes we wear

Here I am, dressed as the pharaoh. I'm wearing the royal crown and a false beard, which show I'm a king.

Last week, I saw the pharaoh in a procession. He was wearing a heavy jeweled collar and a wig. He must have been so hot! Most people in Egypt wear loose clothes made of a light cloth called linen. When I was younger, I didn't wear anything at all.

Let's make a pharaoh's beard

Find 2 lengths of stiff rope about 32 in. (80 cm) long, string, scissors.

1 Tie your 2 pieces of rope together with a knot at one end. Twist them around each other, as shown above. Now tie a knot at the other end.

2 Make a loop at each end large enough to go around your ears. Bind each loop with string, as shown above.

The pharaoh carries a crook to show that he cares for us. His whip, or flail, shows that he can punish us, too.

The pharaoh's clothes

The pharaoh is the best-dressed man in Egypt. His clothes are made of the finest, whitest linen, decorated with gold, turquoise, and other jewels. Like most Egyptians, he has his head shaved and he wears a wig. Sometimes, he wears a false beard, which is the sign of a king.

Men and women

Most men just wear a piece of cloth wrapped around the waist. A nobleman, such as my father, wears a pleated linen skirt, or kilt, and perhaps a cloak in cooler weather. Women wear long, straight dresses or skirts. My mother always wears lots of jewelry, too.

This is Tamyt dressed as the queen. She wears a vulture headdress.

3 Fold the rope in half and start to twist it from the middle as tightly as you can. Now slip the loops over your ears to keep your beard in place.

The queen carries a scepter to show her power.

Making up

Here in Egypt, both men and women wear makeup. My mother and father stain their lips and cheeks red. They color their eyelids green and draw lines around their eyes with a black, sooty makeup called kohl.

The toes of our sandals are curled up to keep out the sand.

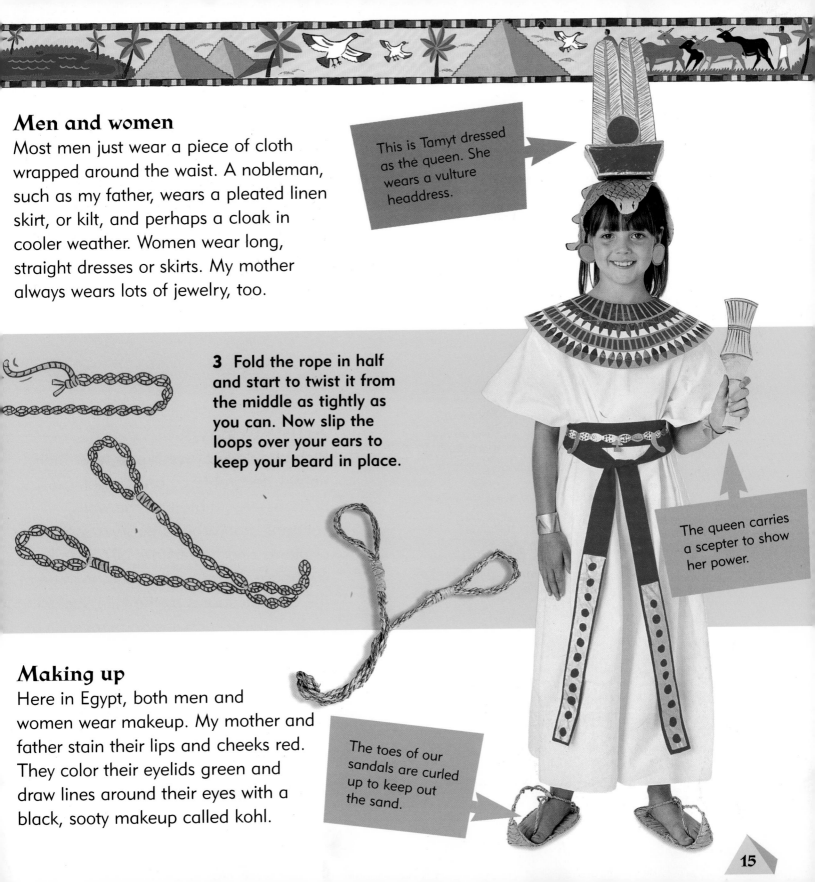

The things we make

Here in Egypt, we have many beautiful things made by artists. There are shiny glass pots for make-up, and jars made from a smooth white stone called alabaster. There are bowls and vases made from beaten copper and bronze, and gold jewelry covered in precious stones.

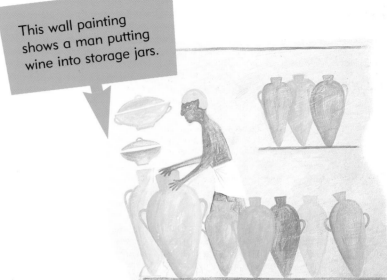

This wall painting shows a man putting wine into storage jars.

My pendant shows the sun god, Re, in the shape of a falcon.

Artists in Egypt

Rich people in Egypt like to have their homes decorated by artists. Colorful patterns are painted on the walls, columns, and around doorways. Pictures of plants and flowers are also popular. In my house, there's a painting of some of the animals found by the Nile, including bulls, hippopotamuses and crocodiles.

Powder paint

To make a painting, the artist draws a dark outline first, then colors in the shape. Paints are made from materials that are ground into powder. For instance, charcoal makes black, and ochre, or colored earth, makes red.

Treasures from the desert

Many of the materials artists use come from the desert. Miners dig up all sorts of useful things there – stone for building temples, and precious stones and metals for making jewelry.

Precious ornaments

Only rich Egyptians wear jewelry made from precious stones. Most people wear inexpensive jewelry made from shells or clay beads. Some types of jewelry are worn to keep us from harm. We call these amulets.

Esmut's necklace has beads shaped like lotus-flower petals.

Let's make a lotus-flower necklace

Find self-hardening clay, wooden skewers, box, paints, paintbrush, about 1 yd. (1 m) gold string, gold thread.

1 Use the clay to mold 18 tube beads, 8 teardrop beads, and 7 petal beads. Make holes in them as shown, with a skewer. Let them dry.

tubes

petals

teardrops

2 Thread the beads on to skewers and balance them across a box. Paint the beads, then let them dry.

3 Add a dot of gold paint to the petal beads, as shown above. Let it dry. Now tie a knot in the string and thread on all the tube and teardrop beads.

4 Knot the string after the last bead. Tie on the petal beads with gold thread, then tie the necklace around your neck. Trim the string to fit.

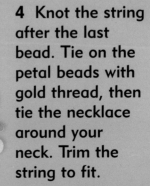

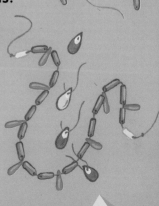

Fun and games

One of the best times of the year is when we celebrate the first harvest. There's music and dancing, and lots to eat and drink – everyone has a wonderful time! During the year, there are many festivals in honor of the gods. Even on ordinary days, Tamyt and I have lots of fun, playing games with our friends.

Having fun outdoors

Sometimes, the whole family goes down to the Nile to have a picnic and swim. My cousin usually comes along too. You can't swim in the Nile because of the crocodiles, so we play leap-frog, or tug-of-war instead. While we play, my father hunts water birds with other noblemen. When the sun goes down, we gather around the riverbank and listen to Father telling stories about the gods.

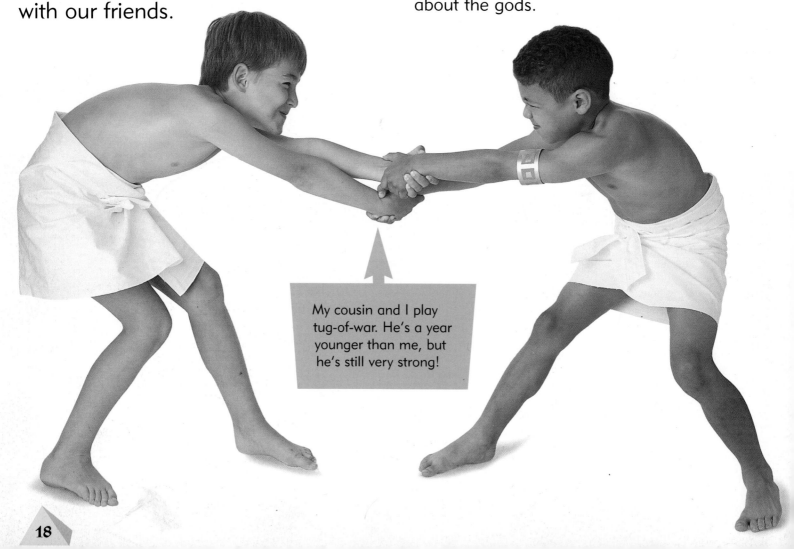

My cousin and I play tug-of-war. He's a year younger than me, but he's still very strong!

Making music

Some days, when I don't have to go to school, I stay at home and practice the flute. Tamyt is learning to play the harp. She's good at dancing and gymnastics, too.

Playing games inside

When it's too hot to play outside, there are plenty of games you can play indoors. Tamyt loves playing with spinning tops and other wooden toys. So does Esmut, when she has time. In the evenings, before bedtime, we play board games. But board games aren't just for children. Everyone plays them, even the pharaoh and the queen!

Esmut can make a top spin longer than anyone else I know.

Let's make spinning tops

Find self-hardening clay, paints, paintbrush.

1 Roll a lump of clay into a ball, then mold it so it's pointed at one end as shown. Try to make the shape as even as possible. Make some long and short tops and find out which top spins best.

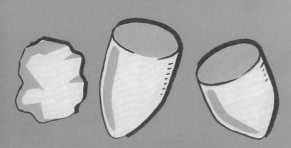

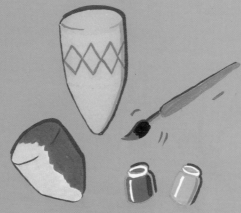

2 Leave the tops in a warm place to dry out thoroughly.

3 Paint your tops with colorful designs. Make sure each color is dry before you paint on another color.

4 To make your top spin, hold it upright on the pointed end and twist it with a flick of your fingers.

How we travel

Nearly everyone in Egypt travels on foot or by boat. You can sail to any town or village because they're all along the Nile. Some rich people, such as my father, have chariots, but there aren't many roads to drive on. If there were roads, they would be washed away when the Nile floods.

Dashing chariots

My father owns lots of horses, which he keeps in a stable next to our house. He often hitches them to his chariot and drives off into the desert. He and his friends go hunting there.

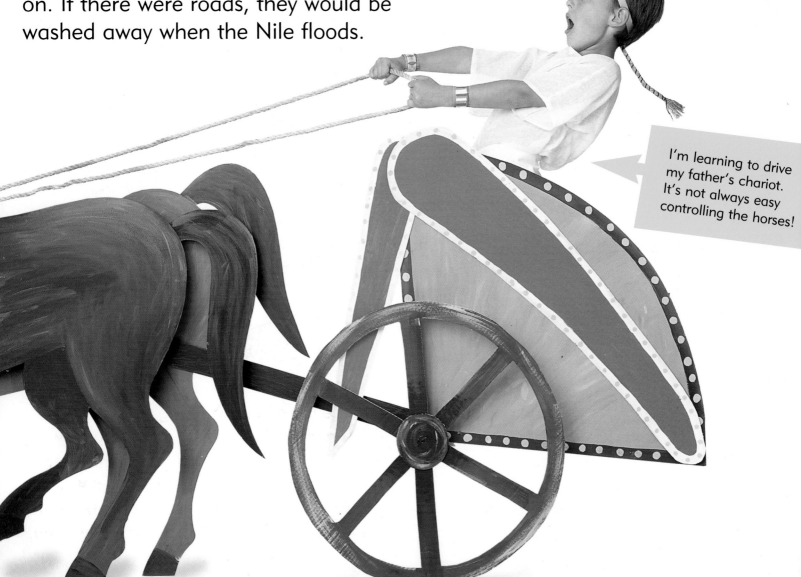

I'm learning to drive my father's chariot. It's not always easy controlling the horses!

When Father goes on business for the pharaoh, he uses a riverboat like this.

These canopies protect the oarsmen from the sun.

In your time...
Egyptians still use sailing boats to transport goods and people along the Nile. The boats are called feluccas.

River travel

Father and I often go down to the river to watch the boats. I like the riverboats best, but there are also cattle boats, huge cargo ships, and lots of ferries crossing from one bank of the Nile to the other. Some evenings, you can even see the pharaoh out on the royal barge.

Sails and oars

The Nile flows from Upper Egypt to the Mediterranean Sea, but the wind blows the other way. So, if you're in a boat traveling to the sea, you use oars to row, and let the current take you. If you're going the other way, you open your sails, and let the wind take you.

During the day, Tamyt stays at home, because girls don't go to school. I go to scribal school, just as my father did when he was a boy. I have to study math, science, and history, but the most important subject is writing. Only a few people in Egypt know how to read and write, and one day I'll be one of them.

It takes a long time to make papyrus scrolls, so we only use them for special documents.

I add water to the powder in my palette, then I dip in my reed pen and write.

Scribal school

My school is at the royal court, in the pharaoh's palace. When I'm fourteen, I'll work as an assistant to an older scribe and learn to write letters and keep records on long papyrus scrolls.

In your time...
Our word paper comes from "papyrus," the name of the reed from which paper was made in ancient Egypt.

Picture words

I'm learning to write using pictures called hieroglyphs. Each hieroglyph stands for a sound, a group of sounds, or a whole word. I have to copy the hieroglyphs over and over again to learn them. It's hard work because there are more than 700 of them!

Royal writing

A cartouche is a royal name written or carved into an oval-shaped stone or jewel. When someone's name is written in a cartouche, we believe that they will be safe forever.

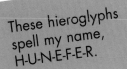

These hieroglyphs spell my name, H-U-N-E-F-E-R.

Our numbers

Tamyt is learning how to count using beads, but I can write numbers in hieroglyphs like these:

I	= 1
∩	= 10
ʆ	= 100
⚱	= 1000

Let's learn some hieroglyphs

Try using these hieroglyphs to write your name. A hieroglyph may stand for more than one letter, depending on what color it is.

a   b   c   d

e   f   g   h

i   j   k   l

m   n   o   p

q   r   s   t

u   v   w   x

y   z

What we believe

My mother says the world is very mysterious and magical, and it's important to make the gods happy because they rule over our lives. Re is the most important. He's god of the sun and creation. Then there's Isis, the goddess of magic, and her brother Osiris, god of the underworld. We go to temples to worship the gods.

Sacred animals

Sometimes, our gods are shown as animals, instead of people. Anubis is often shown as a jackal. He's the god of embalming, which is the special way we prepare a person's body when they die.

This is a statue of the god Anubis. He guards embalmed bodies, or mummies.

I always wear my fish amulet. It's suppose to save me from drowning if I fall in the Nile.

The afterlife

When people die, we believe they go on a journey to a place called the "afterlife." First, they travel to the Hall of Two Truths. There, Anubis weighs their hearts against the Feather of Truth. If they've been good, the god of the underworld, Osiris, takes them safely to a wonderful place called the Field of Reeds. If not, a goddess called the Devourer of the Dead eats up their hearts!

In your time...
People today still wear amulets for good luck. Amulets are often called "lucky charms."

Tamyt is dressed up as a priestess. She's holding a rattle called a sistrum.

Let's make a sistrum ✦ Adult help needed

Find a craft knife, polystyrene foam, glue, scissors, cardboard, tape, paints, paintbrush, awl, hammer, clean metal bottle tops, 2 wooden skewers.

1 Ask an adult to cut 3 pieces of polystyrene foam 8 in. x 1 in. (20 cm x 3 cm) with the craft knife. Glue them together to make a handle.

2 Cut a cardboard strip, 16 in. x 2 in. (40 cm x 5 cm). Bend it into a loop and tape it to the handle. Paint your sistrum to look like wood.

3 Ask an adult to make a hole in the middle of each bottle top using an awl and hammer.

The goddess Isis

Isis is an important goddess. Most people worship her, but only a priestess can go inside one of her temples. The priestess's job is to keep the goddess happy by praising her and singing to her. A priestess also sends special prayers to Isis by rattling a sistrum.

4 Push a skewer through the cardboard. Thread a few bottle tops on it and push it through the other side. Make another row the same way. Cut the points off the ends of the skewers.

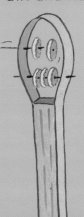

25

Making a mummy

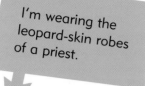

I'm wearing the leopard-skin robes of a priest.

When we die, we believe that we will need our bodies for the afterlife. So we preserve them by turning them into mummies. Then, when we're buried, priests say special prayers to help our bodies reach the afterlife safely.

Let's make a mummy mask

Adult help needed

Find thick cardboard, scissors, pencil, craft knife, tape, glue, paints, paintbrush, string.

1 Draw the mask shape on to cardboard. It must be large enough to cover your face. Copy and cut out the other shapes shown right.

2 Ask an adult to cut out holes for your mouth and eyes, and a triangle for your nose, using the craft knife.

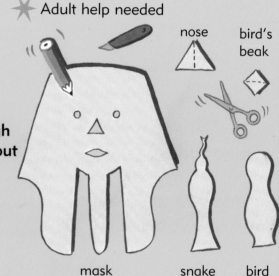

nose

bird's beak

mask   snake   bird

At a funeral, a priest has to say magic spells and burn incense, or perfume.

Making a mummy

When a person dies, embalmers prepare the body by taking out the insides and putting them in jars. Then the body is left to dry in salt for 40 days. Afterward, the embalmers pack the body with linen and sawdust, and rub lotions into the skin. Lastly, the body is wrapped in bandages.

Mummy mask

Embalmers put a mask over the mummy's face. A nobleman's mask is covered with gold. People say that the mask of our last pharaoh, Tutankhamun, was made out of solid gold. A mask is very important – it has eyes and a mouth so the dead person will be able see and breathe in the afterlife.

Eye amulets are wrapped inside the mummy's bandages to protect it.

The scarab beetle is the sign of the sun god.

3 Fold the triangle in half lengthwise. Glue it over the nose hole. Use tape to hold it in place as it dries. Fold and stick the beak to the bird's head. Paint the mask, bird, and snake.

4 Make 2 slits in the mask (where the forehead would be). Slot in the snake and bird. Bend and tape them at the back. Bend the beard too.

5 Tape 2 pieces of string to the back of the mask (roughly where the ears are). Now your mask is ready to wear.

The bird and the snake stand for the goddesses who look after Egypt.

Preparing for the afterlife

Everyone in Egypt is buried with things to use in the afterlife. Useful things include books of prayers and spells, the jars containing a person's insides, food, clothes, statues of servants, and model houses and boats.

Burying the dead

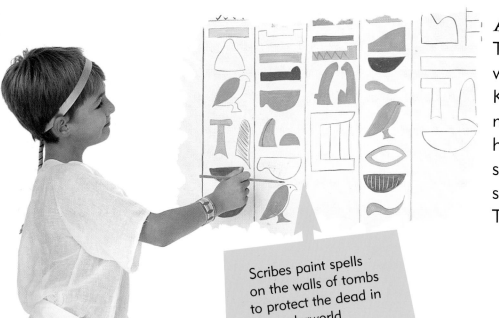

A hundred thousand men

The biggest pyramid in all Egypt was built at Giza for Pharaoh Khufu. It probably took 100,000 men about 20 years to build. I have never seen it, but my father says that it's mostly covered in sand now. He's promised to take Tamyt and me to see it one day.

Scribes paint spells on the walls of tombs to protect the dead in the underworld.

These are the pyramids at Giza. They are guarded by the Sphinx, which is a huge statue with a pharaoh's head and a lion's body.

After they die, most people are buried in the ground, in wooden or reed coffins. After a pharaoh dies, he's buried in a tomb in the Valley of the Kings, which is just across the Nile from Thebes. Long ago, though, pharaohs were buried in huge buildings called pyramids.

The ancient pyramids

There are other pyramids at Giza, too. They all point up toward the sun god, Re. In those days, when a pharaoh died, his mummy was buried in a room deep inside the pyramid, with gold, jewels, furniture, and food for the afterlife. Then the entrance to the pyramid was sealed up so that no one could ever enter it again.

Tomb robbers

When the pharaohs built the pyramids, they tried to make them difficult to break into. Even so, robbers forced their way into many of the pyramids in Giza and stole the treasure. That's why pharaohs are now buried in the Valley of the Kings. Their tombs are cut into cliffs and the secret entrances are harder to find.

When the pyramids were first built, they were glistening white, and their tips were covered in gold.

In your time...
The Great Pyramid of Giza, built more than 4,500 years ago, is still one of the biggest buildings in the world.

Isis and Osiris

Sometimes when we go walking by the river, my father tells me a story. My favorite is the one about the god Osiris and Isis, his sister. I like it because it explains why the Nile floods.

Isis and Osiris

Once upon a time, long ago, the god Osiris was king of Egypt. His sister, the goddess Isis, was the queen. Osiris was a wise, good king and Egypt was a rich and happy country, but Isis and Osiris had a wicked brother, Seth, who was the god of storms. He was jealous of Osiris and secretly wanted to be king himself.

Seth's trick

One day Seth held a great banquet, to which he invited Osiris and Isis. After dinner, Seth ordered his servants to bring out a beautiful chest.

Seth promised that if any man there could fit perfectly inside the chest, then it would be his to keep. Lots of the guests tried, but not one of them fitted exactly. At last it was Osiris's turn. But what he didn't know was that Seth had designed the chest specially, so that only Osiris would fit perfectly inside. As soon as his brother was in the chest, Seth gave a horrible laugh and slammed the lid shut.

Seth's helpers dragged away the chest before anyone could stop them. They threw it into the river and the current carried it away. There was no air inside the chest, so poor Osiris died.

The tears of Isis

It wasn't long before Seth found the chest. This time he cut his brother's body into 14 pieces and hurled them into the Nile. Now Isis had to start searching all over again. One by one, she gathered together the pieces of Osiris's body, weeping bitterly over every one. When she'd found them all, the god Anubis came to her. With the help of Thoth, the god of learning, they bound Osiris's body with bandages and made him a whole man again.

The search for Osiris

For many months, Isis wandered along the Nile, desperate to find the chest. One day she arrived at a palace in a faraway land. Inside the palace was a pillar made from the trunk of a sacred tree. The king of the land said that the tree had grown with amazing speed on the banks of the Nile.

Isis knew at once that this sacred tree must have grown up around the chest – only a godly power could make a tree grow that fast! She begged the king to split open the pillar and, sure enough, there was the precious chest inside. Isis took it back home to Egypt on a ship and hid it as best she could.

Using all her magic, Isis breathed life into her brother, but it couldn't bring him back to life on this earth. Instead, Osiris became god of the underworld, over which he rules to this day. Every year, on the anniversary of his death, Isis weeps for him. Some people say that when the Nile floods, it's overflowing with the tears of Isis as she cries over dear Osiris.

Clues they left

Hunefer's world

Hunefer lived more than 3,000 years ago. Thanks to Egypt's hot, dry climate, many things from ancient Egypt have survived. Over the past few centuries, history detectives, called archaeologists, have uncovered tombs that had not been touched for thousands of years.

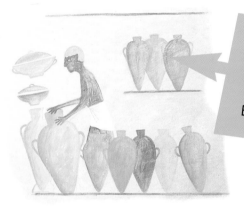

Paintings on the walls of tombs tell us a lot about how the ancient Egyptians lived.

The secret of the tombs

Inside the pyramids and the tombs everything was perfectly preserved. Archaeologists found the mummies of the pharaohs, and all their treasure and belongings for the afterlife. The walls were also covered with beautiful paintings and strange writing. Slowly the archaeologists began to learn about life in ancient Egypt.

Breaking the code

For centuries, people didn't understand the hieroglyphs on the tomb walls. Then, in 1822 a Frenchman, named Champollion broke the code to the hieroglyphs. After that, archaeologists cou read all those ancient Egyptian spells and stories